I AM
MANSA MUSA
KING OF KINGS

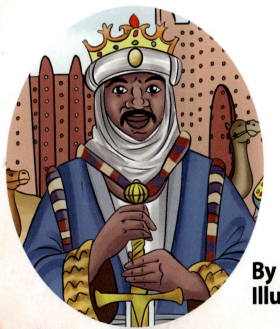

By Amina Phelps
Illustrated by Michelle Phelps

1Brick Publishing, LLC, 2020. All rights reserved
Published by 1Brick Publishing. No part of this book may be reproduced or
copied in any form without written permission from the copyright owner

Printed in the USA
ISBN: 978-1-949303-13-1

This book is dedicated to AJ and TJ and all of
the Black and Brown children
who inspired me to tell our own stories.

Once upon a time in a land far away a little baby boy was born in the Kingdom of Kangaba to King and Queen Keita.
As soon as he entered the world and was placed in the Queens arms she looked into his eyes and knew he was special.
The Queen whispered, "you are destined to be the King of all Kings and will be known all over the world for an eternity."

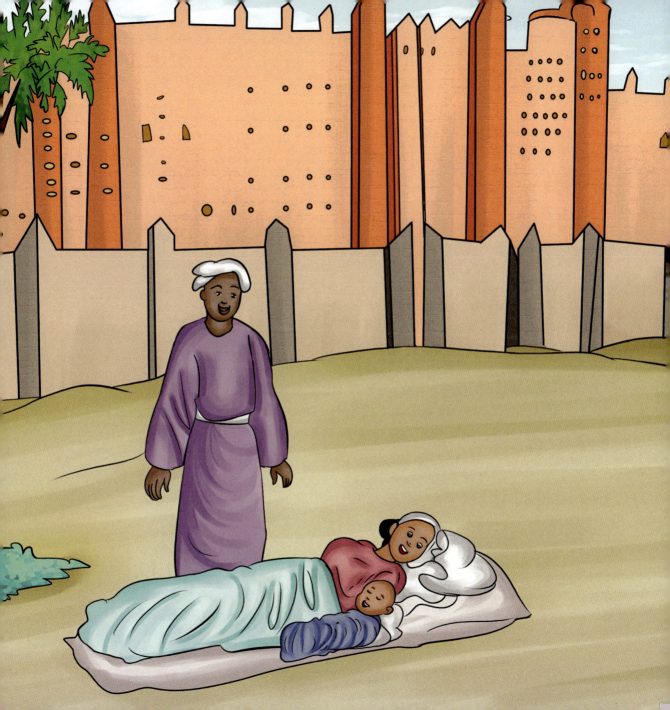

A fews days had passed and the Queen had the perfect name for her son however she could not announce it to her husband and the family. Tradition required parents to wait seven days to name a baby because it is very important that the name given has a good meaning and is reflective of the child. So she just smiled and gave thanks to Allah for the gift he bestowed on them.

The seventh day finally arrived and it was time for the naming ceremony. The entire kingdom was excited and brought all sorts of beautiful gifts made of gold and delicious food and drinks to celebrate.

As the day turned to night and the full moon's light danced on the Niger River both parents raised their son to the sky and said a prayer. "He will be named Musa Keita" the King announced and in that moment one of the greatest Kings to rule Mali was introduced to the world.

Musa was a smart and hardworking boy that always obeyed his parents, studied and respected his elders. He admired his father very much and was always by his side observing as he transformed the small kingdom of Kangaba into the vast and powerful empire of Mali.

Because of this Musa grew to be an even smarter well respected man and was crowned Emperor of Mali. From that day forward he was known as Mansa Musa.

Mansa Musa was a powerful King but he was also known to be generous and just. He created a government that appointed each province to have a governor and each village to have its own mayor to allow the people of the land to manage local problems while Mansa Musa managed the Empire.

Everything was going really well in the Empire. The country was rich with natural resources of gold, salt, granite and limestone. Traders always stopped by Mali because they knew they would be safe and happy with the quality of their trade all because of King Mansa Musa.

The people of the land were prosperous. They were not poor. Mansa Musa was a great believer in spreading and sharing wealth and gave the people of the village many luxury goods. Under King Musa's reign everyone was free to choose their occupation and religion and education was encouraged; unlike some countries where the Emperor dictated how people should live their lives. This made the people in Mali really happy.

One day while walking through one of the villages Musa noticed that many of the people could not read or write. They received an education but everything was being taught orally by a griot.

This made him sad because he respected the West African tradition of storytelling and did not want to change that but he also wanted to give his people the opportunity to become scholars and document their history but how he wondered?

After thinking long and hard his advisers told him not to worry the answer would surely come during his pilgrimage to Mecca. So he gathered his caravan and started his journey to the holy land. As he traveled from one Oasis to the next people looked in amazement as thousands of people from the Mali kingdom including 500 richly dressed servants and 100 camels carried more than 30,000 pounds of gold across Sudan, Egypt and the Red Sea into Mecca. Along the way Mansa Musa gave orders to give away gold as they traveled and word of his incredible wealth spread quickly.

During the last day of the Kings Hajj he figured out exactly what he wanted to do in his Kingdom...build universities! And so it was ordered! With his gold Musa persuaded the best Islamic scholars and builders living in Cairo to follow him back home across the vast Sahara Desert to Timbuktu where they built the world's greatest Universities.

Students from all over the world came to West Africa to study geography, mathematics, medicine, the sciences and islamic religious principles And so as his mother predicted Mansa Musa's accomplishments were not only great but his legacy of being the richest man in the world and the creator of the world's first Universities is still talked about today.

FUN FACTS

→ Musa was a devout Muslim, and his pilgrimage to Mecca made him well-known across northern Africa and the Middle East. To Musa, Islam was "an entry into the cultured world of the Eastern Mediterranean". He would spend much time fostering the growth of the religion within his empire.

→ Allah - God

→ Hajj - Muslim pilgrimage to Mecca that takes place in the last month of the year, and that all Muslims are expected to make at least once during their lifetime.

→ Mansa is a Mandinka word meaning "king of kings" or "emperor". It is particularly associated with the Keita Dynasty of the Mali Empire, which dominated West Africa from the thirteenth to the fifteenth century.

→ Still today Mansa Musa is the richest man who ever lived in history.

Also Available

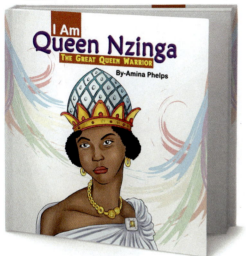

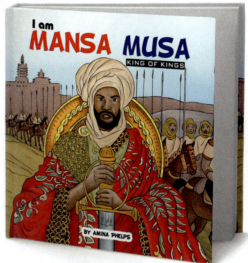

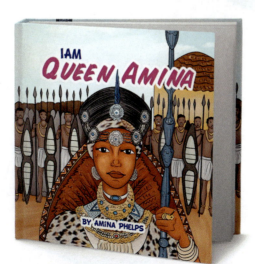

www.IamRoyaltyBooks.com

Also Available

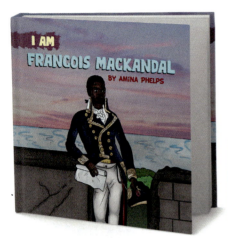

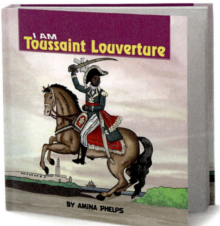

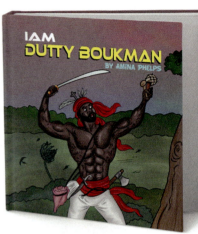

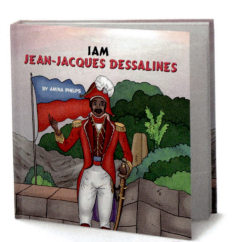

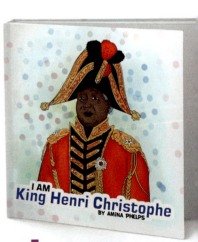

www.IamRoyaltyBooks.com

Also Available

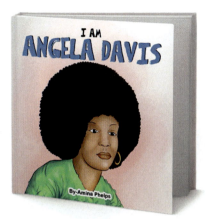

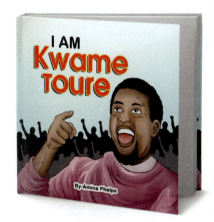

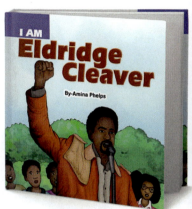

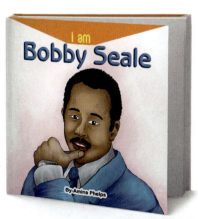

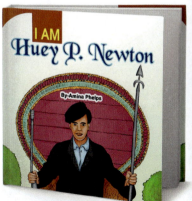

www.IamRoyaltyBooks.com

Made in the USA
Las Vegas, NV
08 May 2025